The Toy Box Ate My Brother

The Toy Box Ate My Brother

Poems by
Jeff Mondak

Illustrations by
Mew Tachibana

JPFK
Champaign, Illinois

The Toy Box Ate My Brother / poems by Jeff Mondak; illustrations by Mew Tachibana

ISBN: 978-0-9972584-0-0 (JPFK)

1. Children's poetry, American. 2. Humorous poetry, American.

© 2016 JPFK

All rights reserved. No part of this book may be reproduced or transmitted in any form or by any means, electronic or mechanical, including photocopying, recording, or using any information storage and retrieval systems, without written permission from the publisher, except in the case of brief quotations embodied in critical articles and reviews. All poems by Jeff Mondak, except "Dear Lunch Lady," by Milo Amundsen and Jeff Mondak. "First Do No Harm" was originally published in Spider Magazine as "Snowman Sniffles" (© 2005 Carus Publishing Group).

Published by JPFK, 4805 Peifer Lane, Champaign, Illinois 61822.

THOUGHTS ON A RAINY DAY

"I don't like heights, I'm scared of lightning.

"This whole trip seems very frightening.

"The sky looks dark, the wind is roaring,

"And everyone I know is pouring.

"I should have worn two parachutes,

"Some gloves, a helmet, and new boots.

"What is going to become of me?

"What if I get lost at sea,

"Or wash away right down some drain,

"Or smash into a window pane?

"I can't be worried, I can't be blue.

"I have a special job to do.

"There it is, I see the ground.

"I'm nearly there, I'm almost down.

"I'm heading for that wishing well.

"Now what was I supposed to yell?

"I remember, it's

"KER-Ploppp!!!"

And so ends the story of one rain drop.

DEAR LITTLE BROTHER

Dear little brother,
My sweetest blessing,
Come play with me
While Daddy's resting.

Here is a game
We both can try:
Let's yell and jump,
And scream and cry.
Let's stomp the floor,
And be our worst.
We'll take turns.

You go first.

UP A TREE

I helped my little brother,
Yes, I helped him climb our tree.
I had to help my brother
'cause my brother's only three.
I helped my little brother,
And I helped without a frown.
There's just one thing I haven't done
—I never helped him *down!*

Y NOT

X and Z I know so well,
And A-E-I-O-U.
I'm expert in both K and L,
Along with P and Q.
I even know that slinky S,
But though I try and try,
I must admit, I must confess
That still I don't know Y.

LOST AT C

Middle C is lost to me.
Oh, where oh where is middle C?
I've found the ones to left and right,
Yes, bass and treble, they're in sight.
But Middle C's a mystery.
It's like a lock without a key.
I've checked my book, I've asked the cat,
I'm looking sharp but falling flat.
Do-re-mi-fa-so-la-ti,
Oh, where oh where is Middle C?

NOBODY KNOWS
WHERE OUR BUS DRIVER GOES

Nobody knows
Where our bus driver goes
While all of us kids are at school.
Does he study the map,
Does he take a nice nap,
Or lazily lounge by the pool?

Nobody knows
Where our bus driver goes
Nor what he may do with his time.
Does he work for the mayor,
Is he off cutting hair,
Or secretly out fighting crime?

Nobody knows
Where our bus driver goes.
He's prob'ly a spaceman from Mars.
But he might be a spy,
Or a rock-n-roll guy
Who's flailing on 'lectric guitars.

Nobody knows
Where our bus driver goes.
He leaves us each morning at eight.
All that we see
Is our bus back at three,
And, boy, we're sure glad he's not late!

THE KITCHEN CLOCK

Those friendly hands let me know
The time has come for my T.V. show.
Big one up, small one down
Means it's time for Bip the Clown.

Bad old hands move on ahead.
It's time for me to go to bed.
From friend to foe, I plainly see
The hands of time have turned on me.

JARRING

I reached inside the cookie jar.
I reached so deep, I reached so far.
No chocolate chips were hiding there.
Except for crumbs, the jar was bare.
I reached inside the cookie jar,
And came away with nothing.

I reached inside the candy jar.
I reached so deep, I reached so far.
No gummy treats were hiding there.
Except for crumbs, the jar was bare.
I reached inside the candy jar,
And came away with nothing.

I reached inside the pickle jar.
I reached so deep, I reached so far.
No chocolate chips were hiding there.
No gummy snacks, it's just not fair.
I reached inside the pickle jar,
And only got a pickle!

HOW I BECAME A BLACK BELT

A week ago Sunday with weather so warm,
Karate class met in the park.
We practiced our kicks, then we studied our form,
And chopped at the sycamore bark.

I sat and I rested beneath that great tree
While Christopher worked on his stance.
My mind was so focused that I didn't see
The ants marching straight up my pants.

The ants in my britches were biting me there.
The bite marks were starting to swell.
I itched, so I kicked and I clawed at the air,
Then spun as I let out a yell.

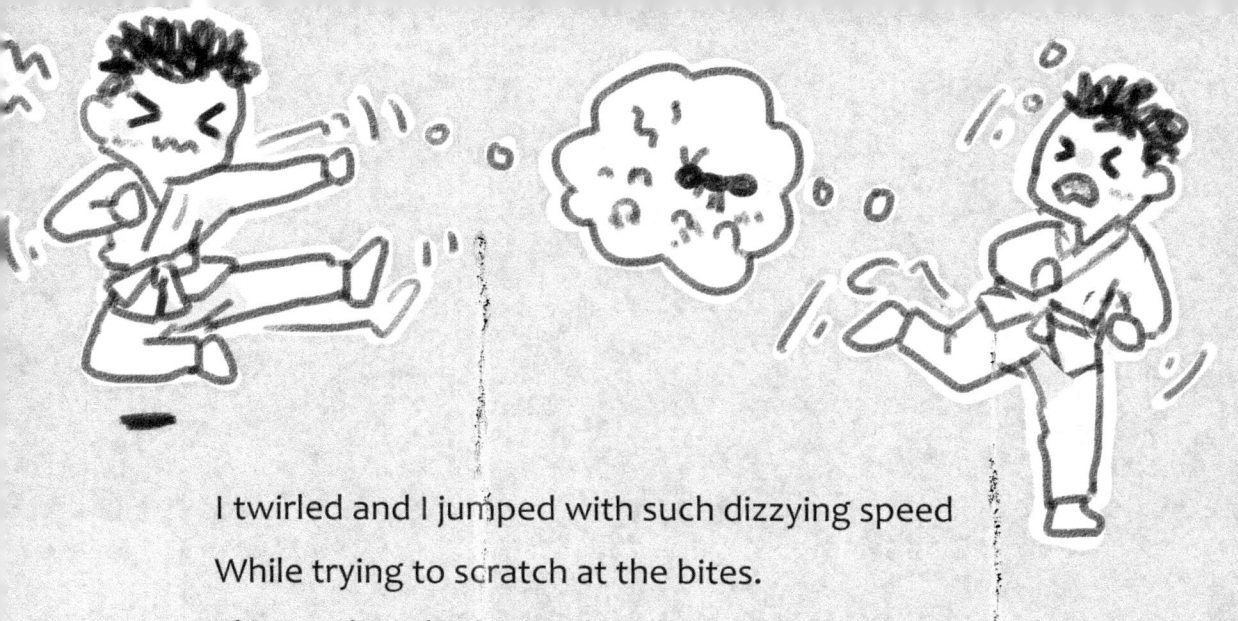

I twirled and I jumped with such dizzying speed
While trying to scratch at the bites.
The teachers look on and then quickly agreed
My skills had reached masterful heights.

For twenty-three minutes I pranced without pause.
I shrieked at each itchy red welt.
I finished at last to the Master's applause.
He bowed and he gave me his belt.

THE KEYS TO THE UNIVERSE

The nervous man across the street
Is searching his front pocket.
And now he's looking near the curb
By where he parked his rocket.
That ship can take him far from here.
In space is where he'll dock it.
But first he's got to find his keys,
Or else he can't unlock it!

FIRST DAY ON THE JOB

"Opts! Sopt! Pots!"
The nervous sign cried.
He felt like a horrible flop.

Blushing bright red,
He called out again,
"What I'm trying to say is
"STOP!"

FOUL COMBINATION

September snacks,
October lunches,
Bananas shriveled
By the bunches.

Encrusted sneakers,
Moldy laces,
A rubber band
From someone's braces.

Decaying insects
Pinned on posters.
A jar with knobs
From sixteen toasters.

A balding toothbrush
Losing bristles.
Spelunking deeper,
Broken whistles.

Oppressive odor,
Gym socks reeking.
Revolting task,
Parole I'm seeking.

My punishment
For missing soccer
Is cleaning out
Our coach's locker.

SHOWER TIME

When I tried to give a bath

To my smelly pet giraffe,

There was more of him to scrub

Than would fit inside our tub.

MISS HELGA GUNTHER REINHOLD SCHMIDT

Miss Helga Gunther Reinhold Schmidt
Has come once more to baby sit.
She towers nearly eight feet tall,
She's gentle like a wrecking ball.
The meanest dogs all run in fear
Whenever Helga Schmidt is near.
With hands that grip like grappling hooks
She holds me down to read me books.
She never gives me food that's sweet
Unless I eat my rice and meat.
And though I like to stay up late,
Miss Helga makes me sleep at eight.
With Helga here I can't be bad,
And so I pleaded with my Dad.
I told him how Miss Helga's mean,
And makes me keep my bedroom clean.
But Dad just didn't understand,
So he rejected my demand.
I cried, I whined, I threw a fit,
Yet here I am with Helga Schmidt.

WHAT DO I KNOW?

Mommy is always asking what do I know…

What do I know
About the yellow
Crayon marks on the wall?

What do I know
About the Jello
That's oozing down the hall?

What do I know
About my big toe
Painted all blue with ink?

What do I know
About the old, slow
Turtle who's in our sink?

What do I know
About the rainbow
Sherbet that's all gone?

What do I know
About the backhoe
That's digging up our lawn?

What do I know
About our dog Bo
Who has been shaved completely bare?

What do I know,
How'd the couch grow
All of that pretty new hair?

What do I know
About the red snow
And where is the spaghetti sauce jar?

What do I know
About the mashed po-
Tatoes that are in Mommmy's car?

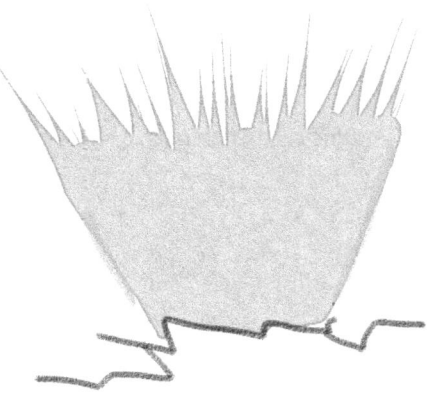

What do I know
About the news show
That wants to film us at four?

What do I know
About the green glow
That's coming from our basement floor?

What do I know
About the Van Gogh
Charged to Mom's credit card?

What do I know
About the rhino
Who's out in our backyard?

What do I know?
Not all that much.
But one thing I know in my heart:
With all of these questions,
Mommy sure must think
That I'm really smart!

I SAW MY TEACHER AT THE BEACH

While sitting in the bleachers
I thought of kids and teachers,
How as a rule, away from school
A teacher's best unseen.

We're with them in our classes,
But not among the masses.
To spot one at the mall or park
Should never be routine.

I saw my teacher at the beach.
I saw my teacher at the beach.
The whole thing took me by surprise.
There wasn't time to shade my eyes.
I saw my teacher at the beach.

Some teachers may have houses,
And kids and dogs and spouses.
But I'm the kind to lose his mind
When one goes driving by.

My head's been set to spinning.
I saw my teacher grinning.
She threw that Frisbee like a pro
When I saw her last July.

I saw my teacher at the beach.
I saw my teacher at the beach.
Congress ought to make a law
To stop the kinds of things I saw.
I saw my teacher at the beach.

Who's to say where they'll appear?
You never know when one is near.
At swimming pools, the corner store,
And maybe knocking at your door.

I saw my teacher at the beach.
I saw my teacher at the beach.
She had to know that it was wrong,
But still she stayed there all day long.

I toss and turn in bed each night,
My dreams are haunted by the sight.
All she's 'sposed to do is teach.
I saw my teacher at the beach.

THINGS I'VE LEARNED

Don't build an ant farm in a paper sack.
Let dogs lick you, but don't lick them back.
Your pants won't fall down if your belt is tight.
Never try to kiss your goldfish goodnight.
Throw your ball inside and something will break.
Make lots of mud pies, but eat Mommy's cake.
Don't push chewing gum up inside your nose.
Don't paint anything on your nicest clothes.
Never, ever try to cut your own hair.
That laughing might mean your pants have a tear.

Although he acts rotten, he's still your little brother.
Hug him when he cries, and love him like no other.

PIPPIN'S PLEA

I like turkey
Piled up high.
Mashed potatoes,
Pumpkin pie.
Gravy please,
I'll take two bowls.
Keep the peas,
But pass the rolls.
Toss it, drop it,
I don't care.
Hungry dog here
Wants his share.

DADDY'S MAKING DINNER

Daddy's making dinner.
I've seen it all before.
French fries black and burning,
And meat loaf on the floor.

Daddy's making dinner.
The sugar bowl just broke.
Fido ate the gravy.
The house has filled with smoke.

Daddy's making dinner,
But I'm not one to moan.
Soon he will surrender
And go pick up the phone.

Daddy made the dinner.
Today's my lucky day.
Dinner's in the trash can,
And pizza's on the way!

THE TOY BOX ATE MY BROTHER

The race was on to get a toy
And Thomas was the winner.
He beat me to the toy box,
But he ended up as dinner.

The toy box ate my brother
'cause he made a tragic blunder.
He entered with a head-first dive
And quickly got pulled under.

He kicked his feet and called my name
While our toy box drooled and slurped.
I knew dear Thomas was no more
When that toy box loudly burped.

No toy box can be trusted,
So I make this solemn promise:
I'll rid the world of all of them
In memory of poor Thomas.

I know you must be frightened,
So I will help you, girls and boys.
Just ship your toy box off to me
--along with all your toys!

SPIDER, SPIDER

Spider, spider, spin your web
And try to catch that nasty gnat.
Do your job and do it well,
But stay away from my new cat!

MY NEW PET

A fly flew in my room today.
I bashed him with a toy.
Now on my wall he'll always stay,
My flat black pride and joy.

He never, ever makes a peep.
He's the very best friend I've got.
He'll guard me when I go to sleep.
I've named my pet fly "Spot."

VISITORS

Johnny's in from Jupiter
And I came here from Venus.
Nineteen eyes and fourteen ears
Is what we've got between us.

My Grandma and Grandpa
Are out of this world.
They hopped in their rocket,
Then quickly they hurled
Past Saturn and Neptune,
Much faster than light.
They left when Mom asked them
To watch me tonight.

FIRST DO NO HARM

My snowman caught a cold today.
His carrot nose was runny.
I fed him Grandma's chicken soup
And tea with milk and honey.
But all this did was make him melt.
He's worse instead of better.
I guess next time I'll skip the soup
And lend him Grandpa's sweater.

CRASH KID'S LAST LEAP

Crash Kid, the skydiving goat
Ruined his skydiving suit.
First he ate his pair of pants,
And then his parachute.

ULNA

Last week I got my skates at last.
The other kids? I whizzed right past!
"Slow down," cried Mom, "That's much too fast!"
Then yesterday I got this cast.

OLIVER'S ONE-MAN BAND

Oliver Oscar Octopus
Is stirring the sea and the sand.
Ollie plays all of the instruments
In "Oliver's One-Man Band."

Oliver's tooting a tuba,
And crashing away on his drum.
Oliver's plucking a banjo
As all of his lobster friends hum.

Oliver bashes the cymbals
While sawing the violin strings.
It sounds like a heavenly choir
When Ollie the Octopus sings.

This song's his famous finale,
A tune called "The Tuna Got Canned"
Now there's a rousing ovation
As Ollie's eight arms get a hand!

ANY ANSWERS?

Our teacher had finished our lesson.
We'd learned about fractions since lunch.
She asked if we had any questions.
I answered her, "Yes, here's a bunch"

"Do horses on islands wear sandals?
"Did Romans have boats that they rowed?
"Are oak trees permitted on Elm Street?
"Can frogs become friends with a toad?"

"Are negative numbers unhappy?
"Do kings wear their crowns when they sleep?
"Does crossing a 't' make it angry,
"And why would a year have to leap?"

"I know they invented the yardstick,
"But how did they measure success?
"And how did they ship all the ponies
"That worked for the Pony Express?"

"If people went fishing on Saturn,
"Would earthworms be useful as bait?
"Are walls sometimes awful in China?
"—the big one they've got there is great!"

"I figure that 'count' is an adverb,
"But when does a noun become pro?
"My dog ate some lightning bugs Tuesday,
"So how come his stomach won't glow?"

My questions went on for an hour.
I stopped when our class was dismissed.
This morning I'm glad that it's Monday
So I can go on with my list.

But here we all sit with no teacher.
Does this put an end to my quest?
Miss Brown's on an unplanned vacation.
She suddenly needed some rest!

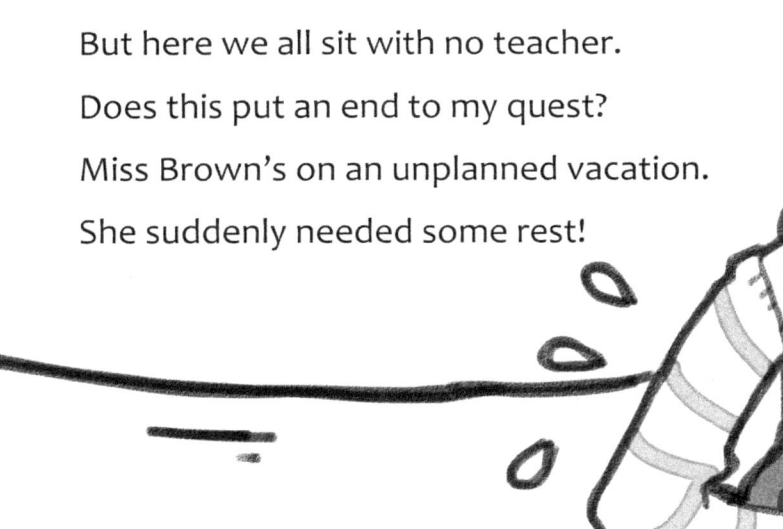

THE LINE

Endless standing,
Endless waiting.
All the kids are
Contemplating.
Puppy, kitten,
Bike, or scooter?
Would he bring a
New computer?
Babies crying,
No one's moving.
Parents grumble,
Disapproving.

Smiling faces,
Tempers mended.
Santa's coffee break
Has ended!

THE NEGOTIATION

I'd trade my brother for a dog,
A comic book or speckled frog,
A pile of dirt, a bag of rocks,
An ice cream cone, some nice new socks.
I see you have some soda pop.
I'm sure that we can make a swap.
Just offer me a candy bar,
A broken tooth, a toy guitar,
A tennis ball, a rubber snake,
A popped balloon, some birthday cake,
A bowling pin, a wagon wheel,
I know that we can make a deal.
The kid must go,
But listen, mister,
I'll never trade him
For your *sister*!

THE MOUNTAIN

It's big enough to block the sun,
This stark, imposing mountain peak.
But it's the one I'm going to climb,
I'll make it if it takes all week.

The foothills mark a narrow path.
I slowly hike that spindly trail.
Although I waiver as I climb,
I dare not think that I might fail.

The mountain towers high above.
I dig and claw with all my might.
My every muscle pleads for rest,
But now, at last, the top's in sight.

A rumbling leaves me terrified.
A quaking makes me lose my grip.
This mountain will not let me win,
So back to earth I slide and slip.

I'm on the ground no worse for wear,
With nothing hurt except my pride.
When I look up, the mountain's gone
'cause Daddy rolled on to his side.

THERE'S A BULLY IN MY LOCKER

There's a bully in my locker,
And it's not a pretty sight.
It's not what he was planning,
But he's stuck inside there tight.

Yes, he's jammed inside my locker
With his bully face so red.
Though this could have been a nightmare,
It's a perfect day instead.

He came to me to bully,
It's the bully thing to do.
But sadly for this bully,
He forgot to tie his shoe.

He came up far too quickly.
First he grunted, then he tripped.
He fell against my locker,
And his bully pants were ripped.

A hundred kids with quarters
See the bully for a fee.
A bully's in my locker,
And it's working fine for me.

SALLY'S FINGERS

Where Sally's stuck her fingers
I surely don't advise.
She's put them in her mouth and nose
And other people's eyes.

She shoved them in a hornet's nest,
And tapped a leopard's spots.
She even dipped her hand in ink,
Then poked some polka-dots.

She pushed on Fluffy's belly
When her dog curled up for naps,
Then grinned with fingers in her ears
To block his howls and yaps.

Sally pecked at everything
With gusto and with flair.
Her parents tried to warn her,
But Sally didn't care.

Then Sally vanished in a flash,
You've surely guessed as much.
She was tempted by a sign that read
"Caution! Do not touch!"

FURIOUS PHILLIP'S FANTASTIC FIND

The batter's name was Jumbo John.
He made his meanest face.
He saw that there were runners on
At first and second base.

He kicked the dirt and tapped the plate,
Then watched our pitcher throw.
John swung, then left it up to fate
How far that blast would go.

The rocket shot went deep to right
Where coach made Phillip play.
Phil saw the ball and turned in fright,
And tried to run away.

We yelled for Phil to catch the ball.
The ball caught him instead.
He never looked or saw it fall,
And bonk him on the head.

The ball went up, Phil tumbled down.
Though stunned, he wasn't hurt.
And while he rubbed his granite crown,
The ball fell on his shirt.

Phil plunked the ball from off his chest.
We heard the umpire shout.
We'd finally risen to the test,
Yes, Jumbo John was out!

The runners both had long since scored,
At least that's what they thought.
But flabbergasted, shocked and floored,
They learned the ball'd been caught!

Then Phillip saw his Mom and Dad
Behind the fence at third.
They'd signed him up and he was mad,
To him, this game's absurd.

Well, Phillip then came storming in
To share his angry wrath.
The runners tried dodge and spin,
But both crossed Phillip's path.

The crash occurred near second base,
A miracle, some say.
For Phillip fell on Matt and Chase
And made a triple play!

An unassisted triple play,
The rarest kind of all.
We rushed at him and yelled "Hoo-ray!"
As Phil held up the ball.

The paper ran Phil's photograph,
But not the final score.
Phillip's proud, so please don't laugh
--we lost 19 to 4.

DEAR LUNCH LADY

You always serve us food to eat.
There's mac-and-cheese and mystery meat.
There's cream of this and cream of that.
The cans have pictures of a cat.

Today it's chicken cordon bletch.
First we eat it, then we wretch.
The green beans are a shade too gray,
But that's not what I'm here to say.

Put a hair net on, put a hair net on!
Come on lady, put a hair net on!
There's hair in my burger and hair in my fries,
The hair everywhere has lost its surprise.
Put a hair net on, put a hair net on!
Come on lady, put a hair net on!

A hair inside my pizza roll!
These follicles, they take a toll.
A lunch that's bald is what I crave.
Spaghetti shouldn't need to shave.

I think it's time to tell your boss
My pudding came with dental floss.
Your ladle work's among the best,
Yet still I have this one request.

Put a hair net on, put a hair net on!
Come on lady, put a hair net on!

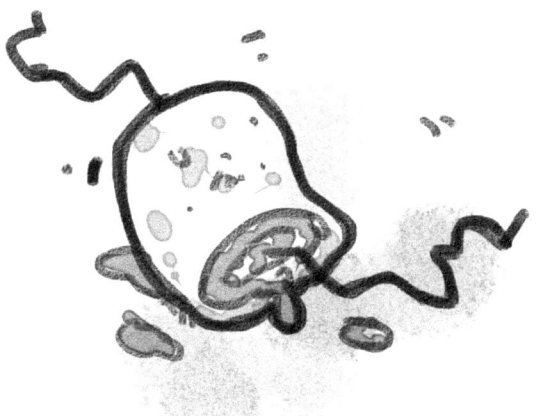

We've followed you through bobs and perms,
I'd rather eat a bowl of worms.
There's me and Sam and Mike and Keith,
We all have hair stuck in our teeth.

Put a hair net on, put a hair net on!
Come on lady, put a hair net on!
There's hair in my burger and hair in my fries,
The hair everywhere has lost its surprise.
Put a hair net on, put a hair net on!
Come on lady, put a hair net on!

MARCH MADNESS

They bounced and passed me all around,
A full-court game of pickle.
Each time they swooshed me through the net,
My backside felt a tickle.

REGARDING LAURIE

My dear loving mother, I write you this letter

In hope that our future together is better.

The problem's much worse than a rash or a blister.

As surely you know, it is Laurie, my sister.

She entered our home, I was never consulted.

In all of these years only bad has resulted.

I'm minding my business, she gets me in trouble.

You're shopping for snacks and the bill's always double.

I'm certain that no one but Laurie's enjoying

The fact that she's loud and extremely annoying.

You say that this summer we'll travel the nation.

We need a solution before our vacation.

The job must be done and it's yours for the doing,

So take care of Laurie, or mother,

I'm suing!

THAT AWFUL FALAFEL WAFFLE

My Mom is on a health food kick.
Last night we ate a tofu brick.
But nothing else makes me as sick
As that awful falafel waffle.

Organic this, organic that,
With not one single gram of fat.
I'd rather eat a baseball bat
Than that awful falafel waffle.

With powdered sugar? That's a joke!
The syrup's made from artichoke.
With just one bite my front tooth broke
On that awful falafel waffle.

Asparagus or Brussels sprouts?
While Mom is choosing, Dad just pouts.
But come tomorrow, no one doubts
It's that awful falafel waffle.

The situation's getting bleak.
My arms are thin, my body's weak.
It makes me gag to hear Mom speak
Of that awful falafel waffle.

I need some meat, and Dad does too.
We sure can't stand granola stew.
But we must leave no trace or clue
Of that awful falafel waffle.

Mom's not looking, so here's our chance.
We're off to eat those fries from France.
And guess what's stuffed in the pockets of my pants?
It's that awful falafel waffle!

THE REASON THAT I'VE GOT NO POEM

This poem was supposed to be a first-person account by my good friend Jen about how she got lost in her messy bedroom and was never seen again. I'm not going to make excuses. There's no point in trying to hide it. The reason that I've got no poem is Jen's not here to write it.

www.ingramcontent.com/pod-product-compliance
Lightning Source LLC
Chambersburg PA
CBHW082225010526
44113CB00037B/2523